# The Gold Tooth
## in the
## Crooked Smile of God

# The Gold Tooth
# in the
# Crooked Smile of God

Douglas Cole

Cover Art by Marcus Cole
Author Photo by Jennifer Merritt
Edited by S.R. Stewart

Attention schools and businesses: for discounted copies on large
orders, please contact the publisher directly.

ISBN: 978-1-947021-52-5

"As I traveled all around the world, I became more and more dissatisfied with my search for God; I couldn't find God wherever I went, couldn't find any meaning, and I realized that I wasn't looking for what everybody else was. I was looking for the gold tooth in God's crooked smile."

—Jim White, *Searching for the Wrong-Eyed Jesus*

# Contents

V

I

# Mind-Moon

"Sometimes, the master is more poetic and compares
the mind of 'emptiness' to the moon, calling it
the mind-moon or the moon of suchness."

-D.T. Suzuki

Light in Frederic Church's "Syria by the Sea"
comes out of a central source unseen.
The foreground ruins are an autobiography.
In "Sunset in the Tropics," the mind strives
to go beyond the dissolving withered tree,
the wasteland in the distance, and the empty
horizon where a brown river flows
from the rich pigments of green earth,
slow-poisoning with cadmium and arsenic.
And by the creation of his last scene,
"The Church of San Diego," color bare,
he would resolve his own pale form
and behold like Eckhart's little point
broken rafters vanishing in true moonlight.

## Jazz

The only way to make it through all
    this is music    listen
heat-bold roaches are taking over the walls
    palm trees swing their radial arms
screams of pleasure rise through the floor
  in the century it takes to crawl to the door
    as a ghost comes from time to time
    to press his face through the window grime

yet that holy saxophone hymn
    lifts you and me
and I say the smoke flowing over the balcony
    has a razor's edge that cuts through
the moon's white eye
    and the paralyzing night

# Black Fish

the hill people trickle in
from their blind hollows
in the back roads under
camouflage tarp covers
deep in the cedar groves

they've come to town
in their finery
and smoke-soaked coats
drinking, laughing
bigger and louder than ever

while beauty appears
and crosses the street
to the Salvation Army
in Morton on Saturday night

# In Those Days

we had no money, lived in
a crappy apartment with walls so thin
you could hear the neighbor snoring.
I'm sure he didn't mind what he heard.

I hocked a pair of family daggers,
grandfather's whale bone chess set,
bought enough beans to get through July.

Mad Mary dancing on the deck,
skin-head Rob cracking a bullwhip,
people coupling and fragmenting
in a particle accelerator of lives—

and when the fires came,
we scattered like cockroaches,
found other rooms in which to sleep
to play to drink and seek oblivion.

Now, the next wave passing,
we're images found in a dresser drawer
the new tenant takes to the trash,
with a knowing glance and eyes
that set another party in motion—

Jane shrinking in her blue room light,
Todd rapping out his next screenplay,
the night smoke and kaleidoscope stars
through which we dance miraculously.

# Old Library

there's nothing lonelier than going
to the library on Sunday afternoon
just to get out of the house
to be around people and not get drunk
or wind up in the brothel down the street

and you hear every throat-clearing
foot-shuffling sound though it's a sad
silent service with few around
but the crazy guy who wants to break
your fingers one at a time
and the children snot-smearing
big picture books while the old
men hunch over greasy magazines

love will never come through that door
and something is missing in all of us
it's a tidy well-disciplined insane asylum
yet here I am reading about a musician I love
his death and everything he created
and how it stays in the wind forever
and keeps giving something to the world

like these old books that whisper
stories of another age and near
death experiences no one will ever read
yet remain the way all things remain
in the vast vault memory of God

# Counsel

I crush out a cigarette
when I see you coming
now my ears are ringing
a soft breeze blows me
right through your kitchen
what a tangled cloverleaf
of chemicals and old shocks
you've been through the ringer
I can see that
but after a little dismantling
post mortem run-down of all
the events that led up to this
you'll be free
and we can go down to the lounge
and forget the whole thing happened

# The Voyagers

Sometimes when I see those drunks in town
I think yeah but everybody's got their drunk
cousin drunk uncle drunk mother father wife
but some of them are just so blown down
blind exposed and passed-out vulnerable
like they're dead or the world isn't real
and they're just waiting for the mother ship
to pick them up from the cosmic landing strip

but then beauty pulls a curtain back
or shows up in worn shoes next to the bed
and without getting into specific dread
look at this as a series of broad strokes
as one asleep under the sun turning blue
wakes up from oblivion without a clue

## Father and Son

My father took us out to the lake.
His friend had a cabin there.
We fished. We swam.
His friend had a son my age,
a big, dumb kid with stupid eyes
and a slow brutish way.

My father and his friend drank
beers and whiskey and smoked cigars.
The mosquitos were thick in the air.
His friend brought out some boxing gloves
and told me and his son to put them on.
I fought the big dumb kid,
while dad's friend hit a bottle with a knife
to start and stop the rounds.

The big kid hit hard. I didn't let on.
I could see my drunk father was proud
that I was sticking it out,
fighting against his friend's son,
that I took a hit and kept on going,
that I fought on with the smell of beer
and cigars, like in a real boxing ring.

# Invisible Land

Hello, Charlie.
Hello, the usual?
I guess so.  I looked around—
the place was empty except for
a couple in a back booth
busy having an affair—
I have no idea why I thought that.
Charlie gave me my drink.
Kinda quiet tonight, I said.
Yeah, maybe it's the weather.
Yeah, I said, maybe.
A big wind was blowing.
It had been blowing all day.
Power was out in parts of the city.
But not here. The last
leaves were ripped to shreds.
This would about do it—
all that gold and red would get
washed right down the street—
back to gray and black for a while.
I wasn't completely without responsibilities.
A dog was barking somewhere.
So it's just wait and think.
I can do a lot of that,
a need fire going in the heart
while we ride the big winds
through the deep black sea

because I'm waiting for beauty
to come through the door
with that inextinguishable spark.

## Western Dream

Crud pours in as workers off third shift
push back from the bar and head to the street
under dawn's harsh light in thin sick clouds
dust settling from cars passing through town
and across the dream river in another state
those left celebrate in the hot green parks
on summer blankets shimmering with magic
because the lightning express is always on time
crossing the starlit plains like a needle of light
to junctions you imagine and more every day
and that's how we go from infinity and back
with no more delays and no sidetracks
the station master rising at every stop
as we climb aboard and he tips his hat

# Implied E

I say, I play a C, there.
He narrows his eyes
and thinks about that for a moment,
then he says, no, no you've got to play the E,
the song lives in the E.
But just listen, I say, and I play it again.
Ah, he says, I hear it, I hear how you sing it,
but you can't imply the E.
He hammers the piano keys.
I strum my guitar and sing.
Tom's kid, Olive, toddles across the room
in a swirl of dogs. Shelley sings along.
We're rockin' and having a fine time.
Then the song is over and we go out back
to smoke and have a few drinks,
and I hang at the edge with the dogs
watching my friends then drift away
out into those dark city streets.
It all dissolves. It was all beautiful.
There was trouble behind it that I carried,
that I know showed in the eyes
or the way a certain note comes through
even if you try to stay true
to the way it's supposed to be played,
the way I drive right through the wall,
the way I fly through that hole in the head,
singing in the key of C
that sounds if you really listen
like the ocean wave tanker chains

fog horn and train whistle morning
you wake up and find I'm gone.

## Monday

That horrible sound of a floor polisher
    a leaf blower    a jack hammer in the cold
dark morning    as we climb onto buses
    and the mortuary burns
and buildings that were never meant to last
    tremble on their blocks
the earth opening beneath us
    as we fall like maple seeds
        into that great black open
            mouth of the void
with believe it or not a sense of relief
    only to drop right back into office cubicles
    with rat droppings on the table tops
and whistles and time clocks
    eyes watching        and big boss saying
            get back to work

# II

## Lila's Bar and Grille

Helicopters are crossing the skies
    talk of another war
I'm waiting through the storm
    in the cool fogbank
among foghorns and seagull cries
    in nowheresville
where the old men hunker
    over coffee cups
behind café windows
    while spiders crawl centuries
from hand to elbow and back again
    lacing another dream
kingdom to catch us all
    those sinister little gods

# The Cycle

we are sucked up
through elevators
we curse
driverless vans
we are worms
eating the world
the bed throws us
into the room
the room throws us
into the yard
the yard into the street
where we collide
and give in to seats
in the subway
crawl through corridors
offering our bones
at dusk
laid out and glowing
thrust into darkness
black holes and
spit out naked
chained and thrashing
gasping and raising
a hand in school
calling a waiter
hailing a cab
bidding farewell
climbing for light

# The Reading Room

He comes out of the rain
and stakes a spot at a corner desk—
He grips in,
hair and clothes dripping with water—
He knows someone's coming
to try and kick him out,
so he lowers his head
and sets up for a siege—

He's locking down under
grim disapproving public looks,
clerks and supervisors
even death itself circling him,
as he holds on waiting, watching,
calling on his ghosts—

# Fukushima Forbidden Zone

Over the black field
a red cloud burns
the boars and the rats infest
the farmhouse by the road
wind never had so much freedom
the rain comes needling
over bulked-up grasses
great roots stab the earth
debris bags twitch
and the forest glows
in one home narrow eyes
feel the terrible energy
radiating from the snow
and know a monster
in the hollow there
with invisible tendrils
snatches up the innocent
strangers who pass
so watch for the signs
on the way as we go

# Thoughts of a Hanged Man

I'll never be cold again
I'll never feel hate again
I'll never be hungry again
I'll never feel fear again
I'll never know pain again
I'll never have nightmares again
I'll never be shamed again
I'll never regret again
I'll never choose badly again
I'll never wait in line again
I'll never

## Sundays

I drive around and smoke
and wonder where my woman is
she doesn't want me today
won't have anything to do with me
here in the block towers of the city
so I cruise by the house I was born in
and see the family that lives there now
like TV people perfect on the lawn
living the life I dreamed I'd live but don't
knowing their bland existence hides
other nasty moods and fury
behind the look of being looked at
pettiness and fear just like the rest of us
so I wish them good luck and drive on

# Oath Keeper

There you are in your sad gondola
I say into your ear
but I come across as wind
or seagulls at morning
or maybe a rusty hinge
because as you know
your younger self never listens
just as now you ignore me
thinking this is an echo or
a dog barking in the next yard

and I'm ripping away all
this gauze it seems
or clouds or birth dust
I'm a fiery angel soldier
waking up in a field hospital
a shark in an algae bloom
a crow climbing the sky
the eye within the eye
so many layers to punch through
to reach you

the train to Reims leaves
from every destination every hour
with passengers in gray stockyards
exchange students with guide books
and even though I love it all
and love this warm resort
where not a single clock works

and everything is available
on the menu of possibilities
blue sea in the palm of my hand

I'm on my way with medicine
and extra change if you need it
enough funds for a return ticket
a little reluctant I'll admit
as the weight wraps round
my light intentions
and I sink down into
the six directions
at crow call dawn again
because you can't break an oath

# Virginia Street

Sometimes at night
I heard the Greek
seminary student
in the apartment above
beating his wife
her terrible screams
or the sound of him
grunting away at love
both always over
within a few minutes

# The Ride

this is to remind myself going out
how fierce the wind can be
how houses torn away piece by piece
radiate seductive energy
with one eye looking back

this is to say
remind me when I'm
pounding at the door
drunk and looking for
a long dead self
the person there who looks
a lot like you should say
move on
there's nothing for you here

and this is how I know
the gray is hopeful possibility
the shore caressed by tides
a welcome scene
and every surge of water
erases the paintings
I dropped overboard
in a grand gesture

this is why I wander
down the beachside strip
among the carnival pioneers
leaning into cantina music

coming from the Altered Case
like a funhouse fueled by
the imaginary grace
I think I see in a glowing face

O ocean I am heading over
undulating waves that say
you need to be reminded
the globe inside your head
shaken and snowing and
splitting open is a good
wind going strong you ride
for fun but not for long

## Bliss II

Can I say I'm happy,
Joyous in fact this morning,
the sun in the clouds out there
to the east over the blue river
and white Cascade range,
and not because anything is better
or different—
the same wolves are still
prowling out of sight—
nothing more has gone my way—
the bridge is loaded
with Wednesday traffic,
and I still get by on little pay
in a vehicle I hope will run
and get me to my destination—
I have passed over now
so many times it's lost its sting—
I say bliss is the gentle mist
and the gentle mist dissipating—
I say the burning page of sky
is a warm wave we ride—
and this Mai Tai I lift to you
is the vacation you've been
dreaming all along—

# Beauty

Beauty is the burned husk of an old house
with a crime scene strip around it
I pass each night on my way to you.
Beauty is the waist-high grass in the yard
and the mower our father left behind.
Oh, and beauty is the white spider web
in the corner of the back door I open
and the sun above I think I came from.
Beauty is a shrouded face in the marketplace,
a deaf-mute handing me a pamphlet
that says Blessed are the Thankful
as I'm picking out an avocado.
Beauty is a beer after the funeral.
Beauty is a good night's sleep.
Beauty is a weekend roll-your-own cigarette
and the empty beach as far as the eye can see.
Beauty is a belief, a mood, a cool attitude,
a crow looking in through the window.
Beauty is winning a scrabble game,
a clear lane at the gym when I go for a swim.
Beauty is a car engine starting in the cold,
green lights, smooth traffic, a job done well,
a dog that greets me when I get home.

# Escape

the armed guards
are standing in the towers
night sweeps round
the moon is a spotlight
fanning out
across the dark fields
I am running
and my shadow shrinks
down to a line
and with a thought
I flash and look up
into that all-seeing eye
and in a few more steps
I find the rope ladder
you threw down for me
and without looking back
I climb out of this world

# III

# The Laugh

There's that laugh
it's a guy's laugh
it's a take-over-the-room laugh
it's elbows and that's the way it is
and dirt under the nails
beer at the Blew Eagle Café
baseball cap and cigarettes laugh
it's a pool shot
and a worn wallet curved
to the shape of the ass
with a flattened condom
and creased pictures of the kids
receipts and credit cards laugh
it's bare trees
and a wave storm demolishing the beach
it's a moving truck loaded to the gills
the woman who got away
and the women just out of reach
trivia night at Cristos bar
notes on a napkin
plans for a screenplay
big dreams in a shot glass
exploding and going nowhere
full of life

# The Fantasy of

a life,
back deck overlooking Hawaii,
a Walter Mitty hero
in the mirror,
beauty and charm and friends,
acclaim and vacations,
exotic bungalow resorts...
       fade out...
and what's left is
the real life of garbage
trucks in the alleyway,
stone cold commute,
a job with shrinking pay,
years slipping away,
face fading into a cloud
and the spirit wandering,
wondering, what's next?

# Mad Alice

She was crazy as a kid, sullen,
quick to take offense, insecure,
invisible, she felt, unless she raged…
My grandfather fell in love with her,
or something in her,
and he wrote stabilizing love letters to her
when she was hospitalized in Bellingham,
all about the house he was building
and its view of the lake.
I don't know if that was even true,
the house, or if he was just painting
a mental picture for her, to try
and bring her out of whatever
whirlwind he'd lost her to…

And who would he have been
if he hadn't been her caregiver
for years, writing in his journals
little notes about the weather
and what they did that day,
but otherwise, silent,
as she sniped on about the Germans
and the Japanese and the draft dodgers
and those low-life protesters—
she'd shoot every one of them—
lost in her home with trinkets
I don't think she even liked,
and plastic runners on the floor
and plastic covers on the couch

and grandfather in his blue
cloud of pipe-smoke—
she ranted year after year and hated
my aunt for her European style,
my mother for her philosophy—

She was an ugly, mean, bitter woman
brooding at Thanksgiving dinners,
put-off by talk she couldn't understand—
And as she aged, it was as if
her own body couldn't stand her, either,
never putting on weight,
vague diagnosis of diverticulitis,
nervous indigestion. She only drank
hot water and liquid opium drops,
and eventually drifted into serene twilight
so that when my father dumped her
in a nursing home, they called her smiley—
smiley—

I met smiley once or twice
in her little room where she sat
and stared hour after hour
and couldn't recognize me when I came.
Then even I abandoned her.
And maybe she saw it coming,
all those years back, saw her isolation,
saw how we fight it out mostly alone—
and who knows what happened to her
back then as a child in that primitive

world of beasts and men,
who knows what happens to most of us.

Hey, grandma, I once asked
on our way to visit Grandfather's grave,
did you and grandpa ever go to church?
Ever talk about the soul, you know,
or what happens when you die?
No, she said, simple and flat.
Never saw any point to it.
None at all.  That's what she said.
Pragmatic, American stoicism,
a grim fortitude of disappointment
and distrust...
thank you, grandmother,
thank you for the blood and the codes

and the patterns for your men,
thank you, thank you smiley—
it's sixty five degrees, mostly cloudy.
Had lunch with Traci,
good Monte Christos at Nordstrom's,
and the forecast is better, surprising
light and occasional happiness.

# Wind Horse

Lung Ta, ripples on the hill
beside the bodies frozen
in mid-step or where they fell,
preserved in perfect fields of ice.

Lung Ta, as if the air took
breath from the lungs only
to give it back again, there
where Hall looked West
into the Cwm,
and felt as cell by cell
his legs wove deep
in the quickening ground.

With each breath he said
"I am coming down,"
into the radio with softer
and softer voice as though
before him he beheld
some beauty more entrancing
than life below the base.

Om Mani, the mountain whispers,
and Padme Hum, for
if you climb as they have climbed,
higher through that
field of burning white,
you'll feel with every shallow
breath and labored step

the plucking at your arm
that is not the pull of wind
alone but the hands of those
who linger in glittering coats of ice
begging you to take them
with you to the summit.

## Sunset Men

love this café by the sea
I come in imagining
I'll pay with dried fish
or drachmas
the old guys lined up
by the fire (soon I'll be)
their trembling hands
holding cups of coffee
could any face contain
more sadness more smirk
they are retired and busy
becoming shadows in chairs
beach coves and willow trees
and clouds floating off
to dream the big dream

# Following a Ghost

I'm following a ghost
up the river
it's the future
but feels like the past
my therapist believes
in magic spells
he says it's a way
that energies pass
here comes the soul
from the barge smoke stack
white plume curling back
don't worry he says
your credit's good with us
and when we reach the source
we reach the general's mouth
issuing orders and destinies
hot tea in a Victorian cup
and a tempest for you and me
brain child burst seed
I am following a ghost
to the mountain peak

# Moment of Clarity

The realization that
we'll never have much money
we'll always drive used cars
we're not getting any stronger
or taller or better at making things happen
while half-talented actors on shit sit-coms
crooked bankers and vile politicians
and tech thieves suck it all away
leaving crumbs for the rest of us
stuck at the kid's table eating leftovers
smelling rich good foods we can't have
seeing beautiful vacation spots in magazines
blue seas and white sand dreams
that we'll never walk through
just work and filthy bathrooms
library books and marginal health
anonymity and oblivion—
thank you O great creator of being
for arthritis and failing vision
for hearing loss and back pain
documentaries about the dark ages
die-offs at the end of the world
black boiling poisonous skies
mean women and the rest

# Wednesday

laid out on the floor
of the Hollywood bathroom

eye witness to the following

the world is so still so quiet
at exactly six o'clock

driving around the point
with a cop car on my tail
I whistle to appear normal

gray and red tile do not art deco make
nor Persian rugs and man-moths

that made sense a minute ago
thought weighs heavy on the soul

text messaging is for children
and cheaters

a photograph says I was here
know what I mean?

we live by too much evidence
so use your imagination

hunger strikes mad money
trial basis shadow of a doubt

mean what?

the scent of your perfume
lingers on my hands when you're gone

Who is this really?

towels hang from the rack
with our shapes still in them

getting closer

I love your smile and your eyes
the troubled years that changed
the images in the art you made

days your commitment wavered
like a boat loosely tethered to a buoy

storms galloping in the trees
limbs bent back in the wind

where you'll go
is where I've been

# Ghost Town

Dust coils into these streets
like snakes rising from the ground,
and I see a prospector emerge,
materializing out of the distance
like a mirage, like a time traveler,
because the old movie marquee,
the sun-white thrift store banner
and the angle-in parking spots,
the slow blinking cross walk lights,
shades cruising the alleyways
while the coffee bums smoke
in clusters outside the faded café—
all move in slow time,
like a newsreel in an empty theater.
It's like you'd have to shake
these bent old drinkers
hunkered down in the bar darkness
to tell them the new century is here,
shouting into their deep well minds
until you realize you're talking
to yourself in a store window,
and the iris narrowing to a black
pupil in the eye is blossoming
white lightning coming your way…

# Give Me a Call When You Wake Up

That ship left years ago.
I dragged around for a while,
showed up at the usual places,
raised my hand when my name was called.
It's an old story: hovering with nostalgia,
pouring over the codes that made us.
Then, I thought, what am I doing?
Why am I hanging around these ruins?

Now, I'm sipping a Mai Tai under a palm tree,
looking at the bluest ocean I've ever seen.
I've got nothing to do, and I like it that way.
I'm just listening to the wind breathe,
splitting clouds with my mind,
having a grand ol' time.

# Time

My son looks back
at me as he
heads to the bus stop
I am already a ghost
and he is far down
the road of his life

# LA Days

When I was young and living in LA,
my life felt just like a movie—
driving my beat-to-shit car
down wide open highways through
Agora and the golden hills of Diamond Bar
like I was back in the Fifties
cruising on Azusa and drinking it up
at The Brass Elephant or The Red Onion
absorbing declensions at Cal Poly,
working at the rat-infested Peanut Company
till I kicked out a belligerent drunk
who won ten thousand in the lottery
and for that the manager fired me—
carving up lines at the Holiday Inn,
having insane conversations with Eddie,
(who looked just like Joe Pescie)
who was on trial for assault
and was now acting as his own lawyer,
saying, I'm smart, why have an overworked,
underpaid public defender fuck things up?
And the weird Zoletoff brothers
wearing their green velvet shirts
and alarm clocks around their necks,
whispering in their made up language
while professor Halsey takes a century
to casually crook a leg on the corner desk—
or afternoon happy hour at Don Carlos'
drinking margaritas in the garden,
winking our way back to the townhouse

where she dives into the blue electric pool
then calls me with a crooked finger
back to our room where we drift high
on a futon in a sun spot on the floor,
stone free and spinning with the world—
or late night drinking with Shonda and Jalal
who fight and fight, and yet he'd say,
I want to have what you have…
as we're knocking back tequila shots
and chopping up the worms,
chasing dragons in the siren night,
till I slip away to grab some sleep
before the hammer of another work day,
lying there breathing, heart beating fast,
mind on the race, helicopters overhead
with lights strafing the neighborhood
and punching through the windows—
so I rise and behold the spine sharp
shivering spears of morning plant life
and the crazy hidden people laughter—
then I'm off to the construction site,
dry mouth      no water—
I must've put in fifty nails with the nail gun
before I realized the futility of all this
and walked off and got a cold beer...
I barely got out of there alive—

And I loved it, was in love,
reading Joyce again and Kafka,
Aldous Huxley and Boethius
and Hemmingway's *Old Man and the Sea,*

trancing out in movies like *Rumblefish*,
*Blue Velvet*, *After Hours* and *Brazil*...
soundtracks and concept albums,
floatin' above it and she was,
under the ruins of a walled city,
LA woman and Babylon sisters,
swatting at flies in the cumquat shade
in the juniper hills of Mount Baldy,
tripping ass with Jack and Lori
in Mckenna and Pitzer Escherscapes,
with vine-heavy moth-covered oaks
and courtyards under floating balconies,
stairways rising to swirling star skies
until a cop appears with his flashlight
shining our eyes,
saying get on out of here—
and Jack's gone off his rocker
because he got a copy of the *Necronomicon,*
and then weird shit started happening,
so he tried to throw it away,
first by tossing it in the alleyway,
yet there it is in the back of his closet
when he wakes up the next day,
and he thinks, ah,
someone's trying to fuck with me...
so he tries to burn it, but it won't burn,
tries ripping it up, but the pages won't tear,
and it's freaking him out,
and he's freaking me out telling me about it,
like our lives are several missing
chapters from *Steppenwolf* or *Demian*

being read into existence through
some magicians incantations,
as we tip into strange cartoon scenes
with giant mini-golf Dutch windmills
that suddenly appear on the freeway,
big blades swinging down...swoosh,
narrowly missing us...swoosh,
as we drive right through a tiny door,
laughing happy into the orange
fire of the setting sun…

And later on the golden beach,
we swim out in the rolling breaks
and on through the oblivion ah ha
neon-lit martini belly of the ocean,
sky dotted with swizzle stick kites
and the moon eye on the perimeter
come to peek in on the world,
and they're decorating Christmas trees
with beer cans for the bonfire,
and Bryan's cooking up a batch of fun,
while Chris plays a strange new song
that slides us into 3 AM and back to dawn—
where we wind up at a trailer park
with uncle Dom crook-backed
and pushing a ratty dog off the couch,
a rattling gold watch on his bony wrist—
tumbling rolling back through Westwood
flowing with the wild children
resolving onto Indian Hill Boulevard,
with street lights slithering scorpion tail

reflections over the hood of the car,
the 10 Freeway loud howling,
and there never is an end to it,
the sound the constant flow of LA,
the eye of the storm twisting its way
in a slouching river rush to be born
like a hurricane or a crashing wave,
or a champagne flute exploding in
a fireplace on a Hollywood stage-set,
an engine revving, a news voice droning,
couples drifting toward the dream
spirit who shows her face
in a rearview mirror as we drive in sync,
linked by karmic DNA,
pulling up to the family garage,
as someone crushes out a cigarette,
and someone looks just like Joan Jet,
and someone's on a beer run,
and someone's showing off their gun,
and anything can happen
when you feel just like Jesus' son,
but we make it through
like a perfect three-point jump-shot
out of nowhere, a prayer in the night,
and so I've come back to tell you
about this dream I had
about a man who goes into a theater
to watch the movie of his life
and all the way through he keeps saying,

I remember that,
or, that never happened,
or...oh, man, I wish I could do that again.

# IV

# Half-Cocked Gun Repair

Come this way
east of the river
the road rising and falling
like a wave
children in a school bus
all look out at once
and not one smile within
something in the land
begins to take over
as pine tree shadows
creep across the trail
going back to a tinker's camp
smoke rising from his fire
and the perimeter marked
by a magic ring of stones
enter and dissolve
and at the crossroads market
bobcat pelts on the walls
cedar shelves of canned goods
hatchets and wood bundles
and blankets enough to start a home
find where the road gives out
at the edge of the lake
the geese laughing in the reeds
and something moving
across the water
eyeless and knowing
working its way back in

# Morgan Street Junction Café, 4 PM on Monday

Wild five-year-old kids tumble in the chairs.
The adolescent girl reads away the afternoon,
avoids her home and everything that's there.
Each of us has a debt to pay the weather.
Today is gray as a movie of London,
greasy-haired workers in buildings of old
black brick and sooty windows Dickens wrote
into the world. And who wrote you, woman,
newspaper trembling in your hands? Or you,
trying to overhear a conversation so quiet
you'd think you stumbled into forest vespers?
Bars exhale their patrons, the street
trebles like a song, and inside every house
when one light goes off, another comes on.

# Rude Mechanicals

The dreams have returned
with their mixed messages—
I know the couples are crazy,
Robin Goodfellow anoints the eyes,
I know the expiration date is coming.
We live by the sea and everything rots.
The sugar hardens to crust.
The guitar strings rust.
The great tree of life spreads its limbs
wide in the middle of the heart,
but it won't show up on an MRI—
through death by a thousand cuts,
love madness and love lost,
need fire burning through the night,
the astronaut I imagine arrives
a thousand years from now,
barely older after his aeon flight,
the way we all return again
from deep space dreams,
young and old and amazed—

# The Contestants

It's a day you might knock
a knuckle out replacing a battery.
It's a day you might get the stove to sing.
We were never more seen or overdue
for this thatch hut version of oblivion,
otherwise known as time-share,
otherwise known as heaven.
Come into the boardroom
and review the options on the vision.
Out the door the storm blows
the wicked and the lawn chairs.
Debris stacks up as post-buffet we swim
through the pool to the sea
in waves that go on endlessly.

# What To Expect When You're Expecting

time and age cut away things we love
people and places fade and memory fades
vision and hearing fade and you find yourself
barely hanging onto the pleasure of coffee
on a cool morning standing on Broadway
or the feel of a good shirt
or the joy of a warm shower
a documentary on the cold war years

early optimism left with hope
for love and hope for better days
hope for a peaceful home
and so we mostly wait for death
one desire left to go in easy sleep
not tangled in the hospital web of
tubes leads and mind-curdling drugs

the next wave is coming
and they don't give a shit about you
they're smug and rich and unconscious
walking over your body to the club
uninterested in your dreams or journeys
because anything you left behind
looks like Easter Island heads to them

but don't feel bad my friend
like you're missing out on anything
because you still have us out here
we're your family in any age

and we've saved a seat for you
and we'll send up a cheer for you
and when you arrive just remember
the drinks are on the house

# Around Midnight

The couple in the bar
sitting by the window,
he's trying to cheer her up,
get her engaged—
she has that look of distance,
disinterest—
a bird lands on a branch outside,
and they don't even notice it—

this old theater
will come down soon,
the faded Egyptian motifs
will go the way of all
empire ruins—
the mummy will stalk
our dreams,
the dead watch from
their loveseats in oblivion—

out back,
no one recognizes me,
that's for sure—
the alleyway is loaded
with darkness,
dogs barking in backyards,
lights, bodies in rooms—

we rush through limbos—
why be in a hurry for sorrow?

Ah—the lure of ecstasy—
for now I rather I am,
and the world will be there
when we get back again
to watery dark coiled
waiting and then—


surprise not such a surprise
that the light is less than the light,
and the weight is more
than I remember,
and the days are chambers of
mercurial weather, smiles,
birds appearing in windows
then gone—

# My Friend's Garage

My friend fixed up his garage like a tiki bar,
with palm tree posters and coconut ashtrays
and bamboo grass along the workbench.
When I go see him, that's where we hang out.
He wrote, "Paradise Cove," over the doorway,
but the paint dripped and the sagging
letters ended up looking a little ghoulish.
"My wife's fucking someone," he told me,
and then he said, "I'm fucking someone, too,
so it all cancels out, don't you think?"
They're too lazy to split and sell the house,
and besides, he's got his garage and says,
"A man's got to have a place he can fart."
A man has to have a place he can rule,
even if it's just a shitty garage like this one.
He drinks a lot, but he's a happy drunk,
glad when you drop by, a drink in hand.
And when you get there, after one or two,
the walls dissolve and the sea air blows in,
you hear the seagulls and the ship-horns,
and you're in a tropical world he's invented,
a sad beautiful little island kingdom.

# Rickets Kid

Each morning as the bus made
that swing around the corner
and we saw him up on a branch
in the tree in the front dirt yard
because someone said he had rickets
and rickets made your bones weak
when he jumped down I'd cringe
thinking he'd land and break a leg
but he'd rise and get on the bus
in his raggedy shirt and sit up front
excited for school while I was full of dread
because when the door opens and we step out
whose yard whose home whose fragile bones
we climb into is a mystery

# Fear

of being alone
of death alone
the hard hours

of forgetting
of being out there free
then sucked backed in

# Teahouse

Inside the teahouse
the old man leans down
over a bowl of soup
like it was salvation,
and for him maybe it is—

I don't know where he's been,
what insults hurled at him,
what disappointments, betrayals,
what treacheries he's endured—

maybe none of these,
but he doesn't look like
someone who's got it made—

he looks more like someone
gut-punched by life,
a lot of years in the ringer
of a cubicle or a loading dock,
an addiction or two,
a couple of marriages
that didn't work out—

so he's ended up here
in the middle of nowhere,
the windows dripping with steam,
the mountain fog sliding down,
swallowing the world,
and he'll order anything
for an excuse to stay inside—

# Hawaii Mind

the sunlit road to the north coast
the white waves coming in
blond beaches and the fry shack
drifters with matted hair and blown-out
eyes on cosmic time        on wave
we arrive out of cities rattled by screens
and wander around in parking lots
carrying our heads like bird cages

thank god for this escape
thank the lead architects
and the soul-poets who gave us
a high-rise view and the blue
pools we dip into broken and torn
and from which we rise renewed

# Alki Point

Oh there was more before that
a break up or two
fragmented years on the strip
in an old room with fireplace maw
like the coal funnel in a great ship
with smoke back-billowing inside
when a big wind hit
so he throws the doors wide open
as smoke and wind collide
swirling and buffeting as if
he were on the deck of disaster
making his way along
all the beachside bars
the only lights on that black road
warm welcome places
in grainy gray drizzle rain
trees like standing people
and he says I'm circling
the drain of something
pill by pill by drink
swilling in a few years deep
sorry to those who were there
because I really wasn't
I was out to sea by then
deck hand at first watch
alarm-sound calling land ho
advancing to engine work
my arms black to the elbows
switching out gaskets and pumps

to keep the whole thing running
captain of my own mutiny
dropped at last alone on this island
as the ship set sail without me
and at night I hear the fog horn
and the warning bells in the distance
running lights flickering farewell
farewell I say
as he makes his way back to his room
and sends messages from time to time
storm glass darkening with mold
and he hunkers in and reads
Thomas Merton and Jim Harrison
catches news of the conflagration
scenes of insane street fighting
crowds busting down the barricades
to rush in and beat each other away
one guy taking off like a running back
with a bag of loot under his arm
and something he swears that sounds
like cheering he can't believe it
world on fire as he tends his fire
the back door open
rain coming down loud sounding like
clapping or frogs smacking cement
and he reads Bukowski and laughs
reads Delillo and spins in the matrix
word chains twisting like DNA strands
down and down he goes and
it all makes a kind of crazy sense
in the moment in a flash

*The Day the Earth Stood Still*
on an old television set
in his cabin at the edge of the woods
with an eager little creek nearby
and a suit of armor on the porch
a thousand nails hammered into it
bones of a dead cat in a jar
marked by a strip of masking tape
with the words *Felinus Extinctus*
a face in the soot begrimed window
and another after that
a flame flaring on a candle
and someone appearing at the door
as he turns and says oh it's you

V

# Nobody's Holding out For Heaven

I wake and find the dog has trashed
the house, chewed a lamp cord
(but didn't get electrocuted),
scattered cushion stuffing, shredded a coat,
demolished the leg of a chair.
He sits head-cocked, with that....what?
look on his countenance.
I move, and he bolts to another room.
The wild belong in the wild, I say,
or in taxidermy on the wall!

I have my coffee and behind it lifetimes
of demolition of my own. How many times
have you been with me at the gates, dog?
I wonder if my debts are paid.
We all deal with the death of the master.
One more atta boy. Here come the sirens.

Sound of hammers, hammers hitting nails,
hammers striking over and over
even after the nails are in—
angry hammering, anger radiating.
Electronics are off, no sound but static,
error messages, the technician on vacation.
Networks of the world are breaking down.

I am light, right now.  I am out of it,
sitting on the shoulder of a dream seed,
a poppy dome, a dandelion sun…free.

Free of anxiety and desire, free of waves
from far away, free of the garbage,
the bill collectors, the free-delivery.
And when she stirs beside me, sheets ripple,
curtains fill with air, clouds assemble,
and I wouldn't have it any other way.

# Interrogation of the Angel

Somewhere north I think
the big woods    gray winter
I was hit by a logging truck
heaven looks like a Ford Falcon
heading up a muddy road
to a green cabin covered in moss
where a woman waits
warm smell of good things inside

and I am a tired traveler
haven't slept in years
tried not to cause harm
now want nothing more
than to sleep in your arms
in a soft cosmic bed

# Psychopomp

I am traveling with my uncle
down this falling apart old road
with chunked out gravel and potholes
an owl watches from the woods
the granite hills burn like buildings
western civilization in meltdown
as heat waves sweep over the prairie
and somewhere over there he says
we'll find the homestead foundation
and a headstone for Percy Wellington
as soldier ghosts appear out of nowhere
my uncle is an old soldier too
come to take him the rest of the way
because this is where I leave off
you fought the good fight I say
they gather 'round him like a cloud
and storm winds roll and lightning strikes
as I return to the land of the living

—for Halvor Legrand Cole

# Madman on the Rooftop

He's crouching down in a corner
on the rooftop parking lot.
"Just leave me alone!
I'm not doing anything!"
People are going to lunch,
going home after early shifts.
The beehive is buzzing.
An I-beam is sweeping
over the street, dangling
at the end of a chain
from the end of crane.
Traffic stacks and flows.
The madman among the madmen
is just another sound,
even when he leaps and falls,
and someone calls,
and the sirens wail,
and the emergency workers
scoop up what's left
and haul it off—
he wanders thin ghost free
and now unseen,
but still ranting, "Leave me alone!
I'm not doing anything!"

## The Hearers

they hear it constantly
a low rumbling
like a truck going by
and it drives them mad
no answer to what it is
industry    electromagnetic pulse
plates of the earth grinding away
and she hears it too
I hear it
can't you hear it?
it won't stop
it's like a nightmare
and we can't wake up
she says it's making her crazy
can't wake up
can't wake up
I say
look at your hands

# The Gray Man

He's never more alive
than when he's stuck in traffic,
heading to work, cussing out
those who cut into his lane,
singing loud to a song he's heard
a thousand times before—
I tell you, you'll see him
again and again, same face
grim in your rearview mirror
or glaring at you from the side
because you're in his way—
you'll see him in the grocery store,
you'll see him in your sleep—
I saw him in Calvary
and once on the late night news,
dragged out of a house in hand cuffs,
popped in the back of a patrol car,
face a bright ugly flash in the window—
and it's always, get out of the way,
what the hell are you doing!
You see, his rage is the sun
those kids lie under
on a summer afternoon,
his calm is the blue amniotic sea
you were born into—
his eyes are a garden of stars
you think you see a pattern in,
and his voice is the wind
that never ends.

# Time of the Greats

my son can sit for hours in his bedroom
he can lie on his bed the whole day
time is going very slowly for him
hearing the screams and the laughter
coming up from the beach
and the palm tree below his window
as it rustles in the breeze with a sound
like someone sharpening knives

I am further out on the wheel
walking the dog up through the park
and what's left of the forest
this place used to be
and then down along the rocky beach
and out to the point
slowing things down a little there
by the waters of the sound
with the waves of light coming down
from the big sun over the mountains

the time of the greats of America is gone
Mohamed Ali Hemingway Miles Davis
Billie Holiday the great generals
great ambition great dreams and great vision
ability to say I am the greatest and believe it
gone and in its place unquiet squabbling
and bickering people in constant irritation
standing in lines overcrowded oversaturated
watching the world die wishing it weren't

my kids traveling through the middle of it
and Thomas I know you get this
I know it registers in your bones

what can I offer?
big death's always been at the door
fin de siècle constant apocalypse
holocaust cold war hot war constant war
terror bombs anthrax
poison gas toxins genetic modifications
resource depletion global warming
economic collapse and environmental decay
it's constant fall and it's never going away
and you have to wade through it
like I wade through it like a shipwreck
survivor clawing through a swamp
sulfurous steaming utterly lost and alone

what can I offer?
before they burn the books again
before Alexandria burns again
before the empires dissolve again
the world again the way again
the beating drum humming machine
asphalt plates crumbling
manhole cover tipping back
as a human hand reaches out
and a faint voice says yes
like the star child space traveler

hurtling through the mystery
at the end of *2001 A Space Odyssey*
by Stanley Kubric now there
that was one of the greats

# You've Done A Good Job

being a pervert lecher
stalker recluse
nitwit gumshoe
nihilist faith healer
cajoler friend
entertainer lecturer
teacher sloth drunk
layabout conjurer daydreamer
builder destroyer
insect toad moonbeam
rock rivulet bloodstain
carpet cleaner nodule
sitcom blurb beggar
third eye zit follicle
electric dashboard
screaming idol tidbit
loose shit reflection
mountain vortex void—
I tell you you've done
a good job now sit down
here in the eternity bar
and let me buy you a drink

# Man of His Age

He was a man of his age,
a little ravaged by whiskey
and bad love,
but he didn't complain,
even under the knife—
and his ghost is wandering
the hospital halls
with an eye for
the good looking nurses.

# Outcast

when everywhere I turn I see a beast
and hallway walls shudder as I pass
as if nothing wanted to make a case
for lawn chairs sinking in the grass
or an insistent moonlit blade of crow
shadow paralyzing every nerve
eyes transfixed by a cockroach floor
believing escape is a dead man's curve
so I cross the border and assume a name
then rent a Main Street room and take
a dishwashing job in a cloud of steam
my life dissolving like grease on a plate
till cops appear with a shot of my face
and I disappear without a trace

# Bryan

My poor mad friend,
once wild hippie San Francisco
child of Haight Ashbury lofts
with blond girlfriend Jenny
and big dog Waldo
walking like a small glorious
happy to be alive family
with his time in the navy
rolling away behind him now
free for all the world
to raise his fist at the demonstration
to say no to blood wars
and to roam the roads and seas
for at heart he is a sailor
going off to Oman and the gulf
to set up big rigs
spinning like clockwork
melting on the shore
and then on through the Red Sea
and down the coast of Africa
to a meeting with malaria
at the wedding of the town prince
he the only white man standing there
in photographs with sunken face
like Marlow or Kurtz
eyes far away
and then back slowly through a dream
on the railway by the blue
sea sweating to the sun

and the black snake of the coast
the fade in and fade out
haunt of fever chills
and blackouts in public rooms
to Paris to meet a friend
who of course immediately sees
how sick he is
and takes him straight to the hospital
to get a shot and recover
and wait three years to clear
recurrence always at his back
like voices in a half-dream
outside the window
on sweltering summer nights
when he's back in California
blaze and golden swale
and the sea at his feet
a great glittering blue
mind of the world
always touching
riding her waves
and now he's selling motorcycles
and making the circuit
of biker bars in Ocean Beach
and El Cajon in the hot
neon palm dream lights
flying the freeways
going to see brother Chris
and his band The Restraints
at the Spirit Club
or friends at the Low Tide

going faster and faster
on his Yamaha 550
the nights reeling through
the ceiling fan spinning
in his basement apartment
tracer sunlight blurring overhead
Cowles Mountain burning
fire spiraling like a second hand
and then an even better job
more money
selling big parts
ball bearings for cranes
transmissions for tractors
and new synthetic drugs
for a wound-tight mind
I'll grow my hair forever
he says
buy a new car and computer
I'm a 21st century man
refitted maxed-out
connected to chatlines
and riding high
with a new girlfriend Betty
cooking crystal for all his friends
the ocean at his back
the railway through the front yard
engine blasting every three hours
and he's blazing
he's flying faster than sound
dancing all night in a blur
and a haze

a never-ending party gone
way outa bounds until
boom
snap
crash
swap-map-check-a-phoo
ugh ugh the bleak morning
the unbearable monochromatic
blue of sky
Where'd the fun go?
Friends moving north
brother marrying and moving north
oh man gotta go to work
everybody wants a piece of me
owner at one corner
salesman at the other
Cliff the parts manager
semi-reliable left hand man
incapable most of the time
losing orders
snap
boom
crack-a-chick-tick-tick
that's it!
I'm gone!
North on the road
north he's going
with his cat in the back
scratching out its fur
road unreeling in a blur
little towns full of hicks

and bigots with their gaze saying
don't let the sun set on yer back here boy
and it lights his mind
with the black night
road ticking white pulse and dash
all the way up the coast
ocean gleaming moonlight
streaming on the beach
at Cape Blanco at last
where he rides the shore
in the silver glow
and receives moonlight
sacred wisdom
Eurantia!
yes
Eurantia!
It comes like enlightenment
like a Blake backyard radiant
vision of pure godfire angels
come down to whisper in his brain:
Eurantia the new land
Eurantia the place of God's children
come outa the maze of Industrial America's
Darwinian nightmare ooze
and Christian work ethic madness
with clean souls
and forbidden knowledge
Eurantia
to live and love
and give what you can
to do what you can

like say fix the old lady's refrigerator
paint some guy's mobile home
ask no price
take only what they offer
even if it's nothing at all
dream it into reality
since reality is only this
make believe dreamland
projection of the mind
yes
it all comes back
from the head of a pin
the voices of the masters
Zenpo speaking from heavenworld
texts of the beautiful all
to our free minds
that wander in and out of bodies
as we choose
or linger on the darklight
hub of whirling fate
waiting to leap in
looking for perfect love partners
entangled there below
hear their cries and go!
And he'll get a boat
and live on it
no tax
no encumbrance of land
no phone or address but the sea
and he tosses the credit cards
tosses the bills

leaves no forwarding address
free free
then temporarily living
out of the back of his truck
in a bayside park
plans bust booming
so that he can't sleep
has a drink     no more speed
pure adrenaline now
and the bay shrouded over
the dreamer on the bodiless rock
and he'll gather others like himself
work on boats
stay far from Uncle Sam's claws
pay no attention to his laws
only the pure godword
spoken directly to the brain
the child knows before his ABC's
and he paces
the park lights humming
something unraveling
shadows full of hunger
and skittering insect forms
and oh no!
the vision is dissolving
No!
dammit        it just won't hold
and now he sees
cockroaches in the stones
his whole sad life
made up of these episodes

fits and starts
and incomplete decisions
Decisions!
he can't decide at all
where to go what to do
but takes his gun
he's got that too
and goes down to the shore
to stand beside
his vast dreamsea
oh sad sad miserable me
a little flea
dreaming he's a saint
or messiah
when all he is
is a mad insect
clawing at the stars
behind which find only decaying
deadflesh
feeding on the wheel
trapped in the bargain
mindwhirl of illusions
roads and rooms and ruin
so he fires a shot
out in the dark
there's a star for you
there's a shooting star
you lovers and sad sailors
rolling on decks and unreal seas
all around
that's my fiery blaze

flashing out up there
so make a wish!

# The Consolation of Philosophy

Not much time left or space,
these are the titanic pages.
You dodged the disaster, didn't you?
It always catches up, meaning,
there is a great ledger book behind things
in which you will find recorded all
your joy and success,
sickness, failure, pleasure and suffering
over the arc of several life-times
(because one is never enough),
as every soul is delivered in exact proportion
the same amount of comedy and tragedy,
so know it today, my friend,
and even in a single lifetime maybe see
for some the balance in the heart of it,
the crux of the great wheel Fortuna!
…as you slide out spinning faster and faster,
heading towards the edge of fling-off—
also note those sad, ugly, wretched, addicted
poisonous and scabrous souls
crawling through their days
or sitting on a city bus beside that clean,
grinning, happy-dull, complacent
everything-goes-right for me
citizen of the universe,
and know they're exploring the same themes
but in different chapters
and will swap roles in the next production
and on and on…

until enough, you say, enough!
I got it! And you will,
so rather than plunge through the blue door
into the grunt-moan dim wet birth room,
you'll back-flip like a deep-sea diver
into your own little convalescent dream,
eternal on a white sand beach
with a thatch hut and occasional friends
and an ever-stocked mini-bar—right?
Or some other urge will grip you,
and you'll scan those passing possibilities
like static stations fast flipping by
until you say—that one
and slip into another lifetime
just for the hell of it,
just because you heard and believed
given a choice between nothing and grief
grief is better to choose,
or you actually, god help you, think
you in your infinitesimal spark
might do some good, nudge the whole works
towards some finer arrangement,
or at least help in however small measure
doing no more than hold someone's hand—
the possibilities, you see, are endless.
We are watching from the hub,
and know from past and future experience
the frustrating and beautiful realities,
and we move among you from time to time
with disengaged amusement,
unattached, curious, close but wise

and wary of the pitfalls
involved in your particular schemes.
The song, the particle, the wave,
the eye, the mind, the raving lunatic
furious buildings and the moments have
a busy and absurd agenda, and you,
you're holding a ticket
and walking up the gangplank,
thrilled and aware of every smell,
every nuance of light,
every face, texture and movement of cloud,
ready for the adventure, beautiful, strange
innocent child,
bless you on your journey,
bless you in your optimism,
bless you, and god's speed—

# Other Books by Douglas Cole

*Bali Poems* (Poetry)

*The Dice Throwers* (Poetry)

*Western Dream* (Poetry)

*Interstate* (Poetry)

*Ghost* (Novella)

# Acknowledgments

I would like to gratefully acknowledge the journals in which these poems first appeared:

"Morgan Street Junction Café, 4 PM Monday,"
    *Adirondack Review*
"Bryan," *Blacktop Passages*
"Old Library," *Chicago Quarterly Review*
"Mad Alice," "Teahouse," *Clover*
"Rude Mechanicals," *Dark Sky Magazine*
"Counsel," *Dr. T.J. Eckleburg Review*
"The Consolation of Philosophy," "Western Dream,"
    *The Galway Review*
"Around Midnight," "My Friend's Garage,"
    *Gertrude Journal*
"Ghost Town," *Lost River*
"Mind-Moon," *The Mid-American Poetry Review*
"Wind Horse," *Mount Hope, Off the Coast*
"Moment of Clarity," *My Favorite Bullet*
"Lila's Bar and Grille," *The Paddock Review*
"Beauty," *Peacock Journal*
"Fukushima Forbidden Zone," "Time of the Greats,"
    "The Voyagers," *Pinyon Review*
"The Laugh," *San Pedro Review*
"The Gray Man," *Seems*
"Jazz," *Sliptstream*
"The Contestants," *Sonic Boom*
"Outcast," *Stoneboat*
"In Those Days," *Tattoo Highway*
"The Cycle," *Texas Review*
"Hawaii Mind," *Tipton Poetry Review*
"Implied E," *THAT*
"Half-Cocked Gun Repair," *Turtle Island*

## Special Thanks

To Rubie for plucking this book from the sea of possibilities. To Summer for her eagle-eye edits. To the existential crew, Tom and Shelley and Clark: thanks for the music and the porch light. To Bryan and Chris, the California connection. To brother Charlie and the good next wave, Marcus and Thomas. And always, Jenn.

# About the Author

**Douglas Cole** has published four collections of poetry and a novella. His work appears in anthologies such as *Best New Writing, Bully Anthology,* and *Coming Off The Line* as well as journals such as *The Chicago Quarterly Review, Chiron, The Galway Review, Red Rock Review, Midwest Quarterly,* and *Slipstream.* He has been nominated twice for a Pushcart and Best of the Net, and has received the Leslie Hunt Memorial Prize in Poetry, judged by T.R. Hummer; the Best of Poetry Award from *Clapboard House*; First Prize in the "Picture Worth 500 Words" from *Tattoo Highway.* His website is douglastcole.com.

# About the Press

Unsolicited Press is a small press in Portland, Oregon. Founded in 2012, the team seeks to publish exemplary poetry, creative nonfiction, and fiction. Learn more at www.unsolicitedpress.com